King Knox and His Knight

by Joyce Mallery
illustrated by Len Epstein

Core Decodable 86

McGraw Hill Education

Bothell, WA • Chicago, IL • Columbus, OH • New York, NY

MHEonline.com

Send all inquiries to:
McGraw-Hill Education
8787 Orion Place
Columbus, OH 43240

ISBN: 978-0-02-144895-1
MHID: 0-02-144895-7

Printed in China

6 7 8 9 10 DSS 27 26 25 24 23

King Knox assigned things for his knight to do. "Tie some knots," he ordered.

"And sharpen this knife," King Knox ordered.
"I don't know how," replied his knight.

"I want you to knit socks," King Knox ordered.
"I don't know how," replied his knight.

King Knox was getting mad. "You don't know much. What do you know?"

The knight got down on his knee.
"I know I don't want to be a knight."

The knight packed a knapsack.
He went away happily.